DOGS SET I

LABRADOR RETRIEVERS

Heidi Mathea

ABDO Publishing Company

visit us at
www.abdopublishing.com

Published by ABDO Publishing Company, 8000 West 78th Street, Edina, Minnesota 55439. Copyright © 2011 by Abdo Consulting Group, Inc. International copyrights reserved in all countries. No part of this book may be reproduced in any form without written permission from the publisher. The Checkerboard Library™ is a trademark and logo of ABDO Publishing Company.

Printed in the United States of America, North Mankato, Minnesota.
042010
092010

 PRINTED ON RECYCLED PAPER

Cover Photo: Animals Animals
Interior Photos: Getty Images pp. 10–11, 16–17; iStockphoto pp. 4, 5; Peter Arnold p. 13; Photolibrary pp. 7, 9, 15, 19, 20–21

Editor: BreAnn Rumsch
Art Direction & Cover Design: Neil Klinepier

Library of Congress Cataloging-in-Publication Data

Mathea, Heidi, 1979-
  Labrador retrievers / Heidi Mathea.
     p. cm. -- (Dogs)
  Includes index.
  ISBN 978-1-61613-407-5
  1. Labrador retriever--Juvenile literature. I. Title.
  SF429.L3M38 2011
  636.752'7--dc22
                        2010013418

CONTENTS

THE DOG FAMILY

Did you know modern dogs descend from the gray wolf? It's true! The wolf is even the ancestor of adorable Labrador retriever puppies.

The relationship between dogs and humans began more than 12,000 years ago. People found that when wolves were tamed, they made good guardians, hunters, and companions. Humans **bred** dogs for certain skills. For example, the Labrador retriever was bred to retrieve game, such as waterfowl. Over time, people created the more than 400 dog **breeds** that exist today. No matter the breed, all dogs belong to the family **Canidae**.

The Labrador retriever remains a capable hunting breed. This dog is also smart and gentle. It lives to please its human family.

The Labrador retriever makes a good pet for an active, loving family.

LABRADOR RETRIEVERS

The Labrador retriever **breed** is from Newfoundland in Canada. There, it helped fishermen haul in nets and catch escaping fish. Over time, the breed was crossed with setters, spaniels, and other retrieving dogs. This improved the Lab's hunting skills.

The **American Kennel Club** recognized the breed in 1917. Today, the Labrador retriever is the most popular dog breed in the United States. Hunters still prize Labs for their strength, **endurance**, and sense of smell. And, families love these dogs for the fine companion pets they are.

Labs love to work and play hard!

What They're Like

People throughout the world enjoy Labrador retrievers. These gentle animals offer love and loyalty. They are great with children and other dogs.

Labs are even tempered, smart, strong, and healthy. For these reasons, they serve as military dogs, police dogs, and guide dogs.

These calm dogs are also useful in disasters. Labs commonly help search and rescue teams. Their strong noses give them the amazing ability to locate people who are trapped. Dust, smoke, and gas cannot stop a Lab on the hunt!

Labs also love to play. They especially enjoy water. These lively dogs are highly trainable. However, they do not make the best guard dogs. An intruder could easily win over a Lab by tossing it a tasty steak!

A Lab won't pass up the chance to go for a swim!

COAT AND COLOR

The Labrador retriever has a short, straight, **dense** coat. The dog's soft undercoat is weather resistant. It provides warmth in cold weather and water.

A Lab's tail is thick at the base and tapers toward the tip. It is covered with the same short, dense coat as the body. This gives the tail a rounded appearance. For this reason, it is often described as an otter tail. A Lab carries its tail high, but not curved over the back.

This popular **breed** comes in three colors. These are black, yellow, and chocolate. Sometimes, Labs have a small patch of white

10

on their chests. Yellow Labs can vary from light cream to fox red. Chocolate Labs range from light to dark chocolate brown.

The three coat colors for Labs are chocolate, yellow, and black. Black is the most common color.

SIZE

Labs are strong, medium sized, and solid. Male Labs stand 22.5 to 24.5 inches (57 to 62 cm) tall at the shoulders. They weigh 65 to 80 pounds (30 to 36 kg). Female Labs are slightly shorter and lighter. They are 21.5 to 23.5 inches (55 to 60 cm) tall and weigh 55 to 70 pounds (25 to 32 kg).

A Lab's broad head holds powerful jaws. The brow is slightly prominent, and the **muzzle** is fairly wide. A healthy Lab has no fleshiness in its cheeks. Its medium-sized ears hang close to its head.

Who can resist the eyes of a sweet Labrador? The eyes are medium in size. They are brown in black and yellow Labs. Chocolate Labs have brown or hazel eyes.

When choosing a puppy, try to meet the parents. This will give you a good idea of how big your puppy will grow. And, you'll get a feel for how it will act.

Friendly eyes give Labs a kind expression people are drawn to. Luckily, Labs are as loving as they look!

CARE

Owning a Labrador retriever is a big commitment. This affectionate dog needs lots of love and attention.

Labs also need exercise to keep from becoming overweight and lazy. They love retrieving games and swimming. These activities are fun for the dogs, and they provide a full workout!

Once or twice a year, a Lab **sheds** its coat. A quick daily brushing will remove the loose hair. A Lab also needs an occasional bath to keep its coat looking beautiful. Its nails may need trimming, too.

To maintain good health, a Lab needs regular visits to a veterinarian. The veterinarian can provide **vaccines**. He or she can also **spay** or **neuter** Lab puppies.

Be sure to wash your Lab with a mild soap designed for its coat.

FEEDING

Strong, stocky Labs need food designed for large-**breed** dogs. A high-quality commercial food will provide good **nutrition**. Your veterinarian can recommend a food that is right for your Lab.

How often should you feed your dog? Young puppies eat three or four small meals a day. By nine months, they need just two meals daily. Many owners feed their adult Labs one large meal a day. As Labs age, they often put

Feed your puppy the same food the breeder used. If you want to switch foods, do so gradually. This will avoid upsetting the puppy's stomach.

on weight. Elderly dogs need less food to maintain a healthy weight.

Avoid giving your Lab table scraps. This will just make it beg for more food. And the dog may become overweight.

Your Lab needs a constant supply of fresh water. Keep the water in a bowl next to your dog's food bowl. Be sure to refill the water often.

THINGS THEY NEED

Labrador retrievers love to spend time with their families. But sometimes, they need a place to rest. A soft dog bed or a crate are great options.

A Lab can live indoors or outdoors. An outside dog needs a warm, dry doghouse for shelter. A large, fenced-in yard will help keep the dog safe.

Labs love to chew, especially when they are puppies. Give your dog a large rubber ball. This will keep your Lab away from your shoes!

A collar and a leash can help owners train their Labs. These items also keep dogs safe on walks. Every owner should attach an identification tag to his or her dog's collar. That way, the owner can be contacted if the dog becomes lost.

Chewing exercises a Lab's jaws and helps release energy.

PUPPIES

After mating, a female dog is **pregnant** for about nine weeks. At birth, her puppies cannot see or hear. They depend completely on their mother. Lab puppies can join their new families when they are eight to ten weeks old.

Do you think a Labrador retriever is the right dog for you? If so, look for a reliable **breeder** or a rescue organization.

A puppy requires a lot of work! Begin training your new pet the same day you bring it home. Over time, expose it to new people and animals. This will help your adorable puppy grow into a sweet adult dog. With plenty of love, you and your Lab will be best friends for years to come.

Healthy Labs live for about 12 years.

GLOSSARY

American Kennel Club - an organization that studies and promotes interest in purebred dogs.

breed - a group of animals sharing the same ancestors and appearance. A breeder is a person who raises animals. Raising animals is often called breeding them.

Canidae (KAN-uh-dee) - the scientific Latin name for the dog family. Members of this family are called canids. They include domestic dogs, wolves, jackals, foxes, and coyotes.

dense - thick or compact.

endurance - the ability to sustain a long, stressful effort or activity.

muzzle - an animal's nose and jaws.

neuter (NOO-tuhr) - to remove a male animal's reproductive organs.

nutrition - that which provides energy and promotes growth, maintenance, and repair.

pregnant - having one or more babies growing within the body.

shed - to cast off hair, feathers, skin, or other coverings or parts by a natural process.

spay - to remove a female animal's reproductive organs.

vaccine (vak-SEEN) - a shot given to prevent illness or disease.

WEB SITES

To learn more about Labrador retrievers, visit ABDO Publishing Company on the World Wide Web at **www.abdopublishing.com**. Web sites about Labrador retrievers are featured on our Book Links page. These links are routinely monitored and updated to provide the most current information available.

INDEX